A Rainbow of Friends

Un arcoíris de amigos

A Rainbow of Friends

Un arcoíris de amigos

P. K. Hallinan

ideals children's books.
Nashville, Tennessee

This book is for
Este libro es para

_____

From
De

_____

ISBN-13: 978-0-8249-5651-6

Published by Ideals Children's Books
An imprint of Ideals Publications
A Guideposts Company
Nashville, Tennessee
www.idealsbooks.com

Color separations by Precision Color Graphics,
Franklin, Wisconsin
Printed and bound in China

Designed by Georgina Chidlow-Rucker
Translation by Jennifer Sychareune

Reg_Jun13_1

To Parents and Teachers:

A Rainbow of Friends, Un arcoíris de amigos, is one of a series of bilingual books specially created by Ideals Children's Books to help children and their parents learn to read both Spanish and English.

Whether the child's native language is English or Spanish, he or she will be able to compare the text and, thus, learn to read both English and Spanish.

Also included at the end of the story are several common words listed in both English and Spanish that the child may review. These include nouns and adjectives, with their gender and number in Spanish, and verbs. In the case of the verbs, the Spanish verbs have the endings that indicate their use in the story.

Parents and teachers will want to use this book as a beginning reader for children who speak either English or Spanish.

A los padres y los maestros:

A Rainbow of Friends, Un arcoíris de amigos, forma parte de una serie de libros bilingües creados especialmente por Ideals Children's Books para ayudar a los niños y a sus padres a aprender a leer tanto en español como en inglés.

Cualquiera sea su idioma materno, inglés o español, el niño podrá comparar el texto y, de este modo, aprender a leer en ambos idiomas.

Al final de la historia también se incluye una lista de palabras comunes en inglés y español que el niño podrá repasar. Dicha lista contiene sustantivos y adjetivos (con su respectivo género y número en español) y verbos. Los verbos en español aparecen conjugados tal como se los utiliza en la historia.

Los padres y los maestros podrán usar esta obra como libro de lectura inicial para niños que hablen inglés o español.

A rainbow of friends is the vision we see
when we think about peace and world harmony.

Un arcoíris de amigos es lo que vemos
cuando pensamos en la paz y armonía del mundo.

Some friends are funny.

Algunos amigos son graciosos.

Some friends are stars.

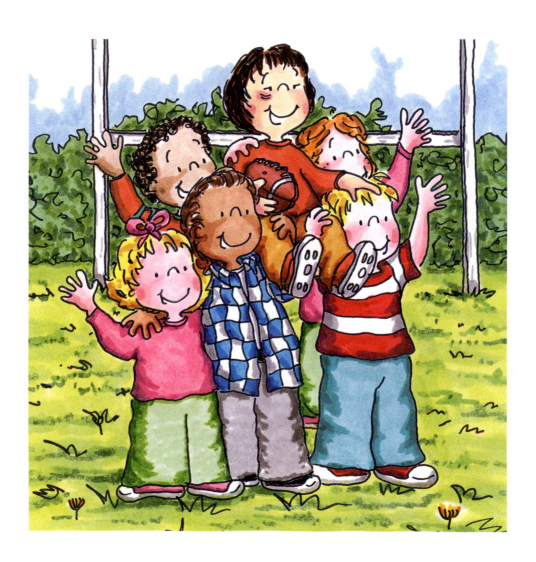

Algunos amigos son estrellas.

Some friends wear clothing that's different than ours.

Algunos amigos llevan ropa distinta a la nuestra.

But all friends are special and add in some way
to the richness of life—how we think, what we say.

Pero todos los amigos son especiales y aumentan de alguna
manera la riqueza de la vida, como pensamos, lo que decimos.

A rainbow of friends is a dream we can share
where everyone's treated with kindness and care.

Un arcoíris de amigos es un sueño que podemos compartir
donde todos son tratados con amabilidad y cariño.

A friend may be challenged in movement or speech.

Un amigo podría tener dificultad

para moverse o hablar.

A friend may be distant or difficult to reach.

Un amigo podría estar distante o no querer que te acerques.

Still, each friend is given a share of our hearts,
so no one feels different, unloved, or apart.

Pero cada amigo tiene una parte de nuestros corazones.
Así nadie se siente distinto, sin amor, o separado.

A rainbow of friends is a chance for us all
to help one another when we stumble or fall.

Un arcoíris de amigos es una oportunidad para que entre todos
podamos ayudarnos cuando tropezamos o nos caemos.

We all have our interests.

Todos tenemos nuestros intereses.

We all have our views.

Todos tenemos nuestros puntos de vista.

We all have our strengths and our weaknesses too.

Todos tenemos nuestras fortalezas
y nuestras debilidades también.

And though we may wander a bit wide or far,
our friends still accept us the way that we are.

Y aunque tengamos un estilo diferente,
nuestros amigos nos aceptarán como somos.

A rainbow of friends is a bonding together
that eases our journey through all kinds of weather.

Un arcoíris de amigos nos une para hacer
más fácil nuestro viaje en todo momento.

If we work hand in hand, all jobs can be done.

Si trabajamos juntos, podemos
terminar cualquier tarea.

If we play as a team, we've already won.

Si jugamos en equipo ya hemos ganado.

Our goals can be reached with the greatest success
by trusting that others are doing their best.

Nuestras metas pueden ser alcanzadas con el éxito más grande
si confiamos en que los demás hacen su mejor esfuerzo.

So reach out with love to the people you meet,
and offer a smile to all those you greet.

Entonces, acércate con amor a la gente que
conoces y ofrece una sonrisa a todos los que saludas.

The world is a family whose happiness
depends on a circle of caring . . .

El mundo es una familia cuya felicidad
depende de un círculo de cariño . . .

on a rainbow of friends.

de un arcoíris de amigos.

Vocabulary words used in
A Rainbow of Friends
Un arcoíris de amigos

English	Spanish	English	Spanish
rainbow	arcoíris	to share	compartir
friends	amigos	treated	tratados
we think	pensamos	kindness	amabilidad
peace	paz	care	cariño
harmony	armonía	movement	moverse
world	del mundo	speech	hablar
funny	graciosos	hearts	corazones
stars	estrellas	without	sin
clothing	ropa	love	amor
different	distinta	separate/apart	separado
all	todos	chance	oportunidad
special	especiales	to help	ayudar
richness	la riqueza	when	cuando
life	la vida	we stumble	tropezamos
we say	decimos	we fall	nos caemos
dream	sueño	interests	intereses
we can	podemos	points of view	puntos de vista

English	Spanish	English	Spanish
strengths	fortalezas	success	el éxito
weaknesses	debilidades	trust	confianza
they will accept	aceptarán	the best	mejor
together	juntos	reach out	acércate
journey	viaje	the people	la gente
we work	trabajamos	you meet	conoces
jobs	tareas	offer	ofrece
we can	podemos	a smile	una sonrisa
we play	jugamos	you greet	saludas
team	equipo	the world	el mundo
we have won	hemos ganado	a family	una familia
goals	metas	happiness	felicidad
reached	alcanzadas	a circle	un círculo